A PLEA

FOR THE

FARMERS' COLLEGE

OF

HAMILTON COUNTY, OHIO,

AND FOR A

REFORMATION IN COLLEGIATE INSTRUCTION;

BEING A REPORT TO THAT INSTITUTION,

MADE JULY 17, 1850.

CINCINNATI:

PRINTED AT THE BEN FRANKLIN PRINTING HOUSE.

1850.

FARMERS' COLLEGE, COLLEGE HILL,
HAMILTON COUNTY, OHIO, JULY 17, 1850.

At a meeting of the Board of Directors of the College, held this day in the Hall of the President, the following Report was read and submitted, by GILES RICHARDS, Chairman of a Committee appointed at the last meeting of the Board; whereupon it was

Resolved, That the Report be accepted and adopted, and that fifteen hundred copies thereof be printed for the use of the Board, and other friends of the Institution, for distribution to the public.

E. M. GREGORY,
President of the Board of Directors.

Attest:
JOHN W. CALDWELL,
Secretary of the Board of Directors.

REPORT.

The Committee appointed to report on the peculiarities in the course of instruction in the "Farmers' College of Hamilton County," its present wants, and its claims upon the beneficence and liberality of the public, submit the following:

In order to present the *peculiarities* in the course of instruction in Farmers' College, the necessity for them; and to shew, that *subserviency to the interests of the few, to the disadvantage of the many*, (without impugning the present conductors of them, is so connected with our higher institutions of learning,) as to require the reform which has already been made to the same abuses in politics, it will be necessary to advert to university education in Great Britain the *idea* which our pilgrim fathers wished to embody in the institutions which they founded, and which, with slight alterations, but without radical changes, has been reverently followed by their successors, in the one hundred and twenty colleges which have been established in this country.

The English universities, originally monastic and ecclesiastic institutions, designed for the education and benefit of the *clergy*, the only educated class during the dark and middle ages, had in the seventeenth century been so modified, with special regard to the educational wants of the British aristocracy, that students in them could prepare themselves for what is termed the learned professions of Theology, Law, and Medicine. The formulas and terms of these professions, with most of the books relating to them, as if to perpetuate the sway of learning over the toiling and producing classes of mankind, were articulated and written in dead languages, the acquisition of which was considered so necessary, that at Cambridge and Oxford in England, a course of study, embracing a term of four years, was almost exclusively devoted to the mathematics and the Greek and Latin classics. We would use no terms of undue disparagement in relation to these institutions; here were educated minds, which, emerging from their cloistered shades, set learning like a city upon a hill that could not be hid, attracting the admiring gaze of the multitude, and such emulation for its advantages and honors, that notwithstanding the discouragement with which it was environed, a galaxy of poets, philosophers, judges and statesmen, shone out, the more brilliant for the surrounding darkness.

The *single college*, which collectively, formed the English university, of which many of our forefathers were graduates, was the model, which, after providing for primary instruction, even before making adequate provision for their physical wants, they took measures to reproduce, as nearly as limited means, and the difference of circumstances in the land of their adoption would permit. We could not expect they would attempt to improve on institutions, they only emulated to copy, and which they held in the highest esteem and veneration. The course of study was limited in theirs, to the branches taught in the English colleges, and until the time of the American revolution, no important changes, and but slight alterations were made in the general system.

With the American Revolution, a new era dawned upon the world, presenting a people in an entirely new position: primary instruction had enabled almost every person to read and write; fellowship in troubles had brought the various grades of mind into close contact; discussions upon all subjects connected with their various interests,—educational, civil, moral and political—were freely made; legislation, based upon free suffrage, had been successfully conducted; and a spirit of liberty, equality, and self-reliance, was embodied among us. A successful issue, after an appeal to arms, confirmed and emboldened us, weakening the restraints of time-honored institutions, and of long cherished opinions. The very point, at which it might be supposed the fountains of learning would be purified, and made to subserve an order of things, in many respects opposed to the sanctions, precedents, and doctrines, they had so long inculcated: but no—the *men* were released, whom filial loyalty had bound to servitude; while they honored the *mother*, by leaving to her own reflections the propriety of amending her teachings. In their litany they struck out King, and inserted President, leaving free discussion to combat other assumptions. This is not the occasion, had we the ability, to portray the deep and radical changes which man, thinking and acting in freedom and intelligence, will be sure to require; we have only to do with what we consider unwarrantable, though almost universal prejudice, in favor of particular studies, proper for the few, to the injury of the general diffusion of knowledge to the many, so pertinaciously adhered to, as to react injuriously upon the institutions themselves, so that for many years past, our higher institutions of learning, amid general prosperity, a high appreciation of learning, and the vast and increasing requirements for it, are in an embarrassed and declining condition, not themselves performing the use which is required, and practically standing in the way of other institutions being established.

Consider the prominence which a knowledge of the dead languages, and of ancient classical literature, must have held, as a *necessary* part of education, and which is but slightly weakened among the learned of the present day,—when a whole people, having politically renounced *one the sovereign*, and given cordial and unqualified adhesion to *all the sover-*

eign, ever requiring to be instructed in their high duties, when, notwithstanding there were governments to establish upon entire new principles, a country teeming with *undeveloped* resources, inexhaustible in its *latent* wealth, a virgin soil adapted to the production of all the necessaries and luxuries of life, and of the great staples of commerce, *lying idle,* to be cultivated, lands to be surveyed and cleared, roads and bridges to be constructed, ships to be built and navigated, systems of finance to be contrived, manufactories to be established, mines to be wrought; in a word, "all the means which science has provided to aid in the march of civilization," to be employed; and so far as our colleges were concerned, when the ardent freeman sought for himself or his sons, among their quiet shades, to procure the aid of learned professors, to qualify them for duties necessary to be performed, and which they were ambitious to accomplish, lacking only the science to direct,—repulsed,—because they had not expended their time and energies, upon a sufficient number of Greek and Latin verbs,—as though Homer and Demosthenes, Virgil and Horace, were the substratum of republican government, and lay at the foundation for developing the resources of this new and vast continent.

In answer to the question, what should be the proper education of a man?—the view presents itself,—that he is not placed on this mundane sphere merely "to fume and fret his hour upon its stage," and then to be no more. Even though extended to more than three-score years and ten, it comprehends but a minute, though important portion of life—*Immortality, Eternity*—though our conceptions are entirely inadequate to comprehend the vastness of the terms, we profess faith in them, and that they are justly applicable to *our lives,* which we believe uncircumscribed but with their duration.—Where is the college, except as a mere exercise in gauging the acquisition of language, that requires an examination in the documents of the Christian religion? emphatically the religion of our people,—the revelation of immortality, the rule of life,—a religion, which is the foundation of government, the basis of law, the cement of society;—the *only religion* that is spiritual, intellectual and moral,—adapted to the simple in his simplicity, and to the wise in his wisdom,—teaching the most enlightened duty and the most enlarged usefulness. So far from denying, all our institutions of learning would acknowledge, and even add to the paramount importance of the OLD AND NEW TESTAMENT; and yet, without requiring a knowledge of them for introduction to an academic course, or for college honors, they require youth, in the plastic age, when impressions are most vivid and lasting, to spend a year or more in the study of the "proud, destructive, unforgiving virtues of Greek and Roman patriots," portrayed in all the graces of language and the fascinations of poetry—a longer time, under their tuition, to inculcate their primary importance.—The assertion by Martin Luther, and his appeal to *them*, that the *Christian Scriptures* did not authorize the means taken for decoration of the *temples of religion*, an emulation of one of the classic arts, set the world in a blaze, caused a reformation in religion, and the revival of learning.—What may we not expect, from further appeals to them, against errors and corruptions in high, and misery and destitution in low places, when, leaving traditions and precedents, their importance is acknowledged, and the letter and spirit of their doctrines studied from *them*, as a text book, in our higher institutions of learning? Agrarianism, Owenism, the many forms of socialism, and a thousand independent moral panaceas, would not be obtruding their vain specifics, to *perfect health*, which can be obtained and continued only at this source.

We can account for this apathy, only by reasons which prove the glorious perfection it is acting against. The ever-acting sun, the central and immediate cause of natural vision, vegetation and life, so evident and constant, is less regarded than brief, casual, and unimportant manifestations.—Differing sects have each striven for the control of these institutions, and when obtained, have endeavored to engraft peculiarities, without transplanting and nurturing *the root* into the soil, where it would best grow and produce fruit,—requiring the time and energies of students to be directed to the ancient classics, more or less at least, to the exclusion of knowledge required by the wants of the community, and the spirit of the age in which we live—to the attainment of a *Christian and American education.*

A writer in the Edinburgh Review, (April, 1849,) in relation to the ancient classics and mathematics, says :—"But even as a preparatory training, is the actual benefit ever found to justify their high pretensions ? Is there any man alive who can say, not with truth, but even with conviction, that the best and most laborious scholars and mathematicians of the university are the best lawyers, physicians, philosophers or statesmen of England ? The very reverse is the plain, if not the acknowledged fact. It would be difficult to find at present, among the most eminent leaders of Westminster Hall, any whose academical course was distinguished by studies or crowned with honors, either mathematical or classical. The extent to which academical distinctions have latterly been thrown in the back ground, in the professional and public life of England, has gone lengths which really surprise us."

We suppose the truths of these remarks are equally obvious in this country. How many have risen to distinguished usefulness, without having entered the walls of a college, though they have held almost a monopoly for instruction in the branches necessary for professional and public duties !

The average of human life is not perhaps over thirty years, one-sixth to an eighth of which, by the system pursued in our colleges, is consumed in the acquisition of dead languages, in after life now so little used, even in "the professions," that it is not uncommon to hear persons, after ten or twenty years of active and successful practice in them, say, they could not successfully sustain an examination for admission into the college from which they graduated; and the more active and stern have been their duties, the more likely they would be to prove the truth of the observation.

We would not decry a classical education, or prevent those who choose, from drinking deeper at the fountains of it, than any now do. As a superstructure upon a proper foundation, it elevates the thoughts, improves the taste, emboldens, we might almost say, humanizes the affections, and what is of more consequence, tends to ennoble the actions. But these are not now altogether buried in the dead languages, and the advocates for retaining the high position claimed for them, as a *necessary part of a liberal education*, can justly urge, only the difference between the words in the language in which they were actually written, and translations into our mother tongue; the collateral advantages of a knowledge of the dead languages, although important, would not seem to make the study of them so *universally indispensable.* May it not be, that the voluptuous graces of beautiful mythology, have a tendency to attract young attention from wise theology; and that while we are so tenaciously clinging to, and upholding, an ancient, classical, very apparent, but *Ptolemaic* literature, we practically prevent the introduction of modern *Copernican* truth, to be illustrated by its Kepler, Newton and La Place, and made worthy to supercede it? Those who read and understand Shakspeare, who did not suppose his works worthy of being collated, Milton, to whom ten pounds was a remuneration for "Paradise Lost," Junius, afraid or ashamed to be known, may answer. Of Johsons, Goldsmiths, and Eleazer Smiths,

2

we say nothing. But allowing their importance,—by a just division of labor, may it not be, that some kindred genius, in view of the greater want which will thus be occasioned, and the increased ability to supply it, will embody *in living language* those forms of thought and expression which have been the wonder and admiration of long succeeding ages? The Church even, was never forbidden to borrow *jewels* of the Egyptians.

An examination of the course of studies in all our colleges, will show, that a very large portion, really requiring more time to master them, than the four years allotted to the whole college course, is devoted to studies, having none, or very remote relation to the active duties of life. It is not the first time the assertion has been hazarded, that the single academy at West Point, has done more to advance the physical improvement of our country, certainly in its canals and railroads, than all our colleges united.

Some encouragement is found in the signs of the times, that a reformation in the course of collegiate education is at hand. Many colleges have, in aid of their funds, found it necessary to submit to a scientific department connected with them, but so entirely subordinate, in the view of professors and pupils, that the one consider it an incumbrance, and the other almost feel disgraced,—showing the want, but practically discouraging other than the regular course. A brighter sign is, that Harvard University has accepted the munificent donation of $100,000 from Abbott Lawrence, to establish a college upon reformed principles as an adjunct to theirs, where the manufacturer, mechanic, engineer, and perhaps merchant, may be educated for the duties pertaining to their occupations. And that Brown University has instituted an inquiry, which from a high source has been answered favorable to a radical change in their whole course.*

* It would really be curious to examine into the birth and progress of the English language, and to conjecture when it will be thought to be able to go

So far as we know, the idea that a change was necessary in the course of instruction pursued in our colleges, particularly in regard to making a knowledge of the dead languages, and the pure mathematics, indispensable to admission to their advantages, and to a participation of their honors, it was first broached by Thomas S. Grimke, himself an elegant and accurate classical scholar, of whom Mr. Mansfield, in a biographical sketch of him, says, "to the classics he appears to have devoted a double attention, first studying them in the ordinary way, and then using them in connection with his own vigorous intellect, to prove the language and literature of ancient Greece and Rome inconsistent with and unnecessary, and alien to the Christian system." Mr. Grimke introduced the subject in some notes published in his native city of Charleston, S. C.; enlarged upon them in an addresss

alone. From Chaucer down, it has been imbued with so much soul, or at least mental vitality, that there are few probably who fear its premature death. When it is out of the leading-strings of its timid nurses, it may do more, and greater things, than at present is thought of. That it is beginning to talk pretty well, we have abundant evidence. Even "the professions" have not that repugnance to its use in important matters, as formerly. Though in Christendom a majority of the clergy may continue to use Latin in their worship, so far as we know, the vernacular is used by all of the reformed. Learned M. D.'s, though they may adhere to unintelligible zig-zag, black letter prescriptions, send their bills in very plain English. The love the lawyers bear to learning is in fault, that they will use Latin where English would serve as well, notwithstanding a precedent stated by Lord Campbell at variance, and going to the other extreme, that in 1820 or there-abouts, a Welsh judge, on a trial for murder, ruled "that the indictment and the evidence, must not be interpreted into Welsh for the information of the prisoner, as that would be contrary to the statute of George II., which requires all proceedings to be carried on in the English language." It is, however, comparatively of late date, when all legal proceedings were in dead languages. Styles, reporter of decisions in the court of king's bench, thus laments, in 1658, "I have made these reports speak English, not that I believe they will be thereby generally made more useful, for I have always and yet am of opinion that that part of the common law which is in English, hath only occasioned the making unquiet spirits, contentiously knowing, and more apt to offend others than to defend themselves, but I have done it in obedience to authority." The authority was an ordinance of Cromwell's parliament. As late as 1730, all indictments and special verdicts were in Latin, and in a debate in the English House of Lords in 1731, Lord Raymond, Chief Justice of King's Bench, made a speech, opposing the use o the English language in legal proceedings.

delivered at the commencement of Oxford College, in Ohio, in 1834, reiterated and went at large into the argument in an address before the Western Literary Institute and College of Professional Teachers, at their annual meeting in Cincinnati, in 1834, which was printed with the transactions of that institution. He there gives it as "the fruits of reading and meditation, of conversation and observation, through a period of twenty-seven years, that there must be an American revolution in education, before it will be fit and worthy of this country."

Francis Wayland, President of Brown University, whose opinions and reasoning give direction and force to many of the ideas herein adduced, in an elaborate report, made to the trustees of Brown University in March of the present year, though he argues the point mainly as an economic arrangement, suited to the wants of the colleges and the public, we gladly refer to, and would like it to be in the hands of every one, "to illustrate the tendency of a system of education raised by great endowments above the control of enlightened public opinion." After a careful examination of the statistics of the colleges in New England, where a liberal education is more highly appreciated than in any other part of our country, including in his estimates, Bowdoin, Waterville, Dartmouth, Middlebury, University of Vermont, Williams, Amherst, Harvard, Brown, Trinity, Yale, and Wesleyan University, he comes to the conclusion, that since 1830, though the population of New England has increased from 1,955,207 to 2,800,000, her capital doubled or even trebled in that period, and the number of persons able to avail themselves of a collegiate education is increased in a similar proportion; though very large sums have been given to sustain the colleges, and the means of education in all of them greatly enlarged; that in 1830, one in 13,650 of the population of New England was pursuing a collegiate education, and in 1849, only one in 14,080, showing that "the number of those seeking a collegiate education is actually growing less, at a time when the subject of education has attracted the attention of the whole community to a degree altogether unprecedented in their history;" and that the diminution of members in their own institution, has "continued for so long a period, and with so steady a progress, that he is forced to a conclusion that its causes are permanent."

The arguments, conclusions and recommendations of President Wayland, if copied, would furnish stronger reasons for the peculiarities in the course of instruction in Farmers' College, than any which we could adduce. We copy the following, all pointing to that peculiarity: "Except the *ancient languages*, there are but few of the studies now pursued in college, which if well taught would not be attractive to young men preparing for any of the departments of life." "Many young men who intend to enter the professions, are unwilling, or unable, to spend *four years* in the preparatory studies of college; they would, however, cheerfully spend one or two years in such study, if they were allowed to select such *branches of science as they chose.*" "The present system of adjusting collegiate study to a fixed term of four years, *or to any other term*, must be abandoned, and every student allowed, within limits to be determined by statute, to carry on, at the same time, a greater or less number of courses as he may choose."—"That the time allotted to any particular course of instruction should be determined by the *nature of the course itself*, and not by its supposed relation to the wants of any particular profession." "That the various courses should be so arranged, that, in so far as is practicable, every student might study *what he chose*, all that he chose, and *nothing but what he chose.* The faculty, however, at the request of a parent or guardian, should have authority to assign to their student such a course as they might deem for his advantage."—"That every student should be entitled to a certificate of such proficiency as he may have made in every course pursued."

In the course of his reasoning that the change is *just, expedient, and necessary,* he says, "our institutions of learning have generally been endowed by the wealth of the producing classes of society. It is surely unjust that a system should be *universally* adopted, which practically excludes them from the benefits which they have conferred upon others," and that, "if every man who is willing to pay for them, has an *equal* right to the benefits of education, every man has a *special* right to that kind of education which will be of greatest value to him in the prosecution of useful industry, it is therefore eminently unjust, practically to exclude the largest class of the community from an opportunity of acquiring that knowledge, the possession of which is of inestimable importance, both to national progress and individual success; and yet we have in this country 120 colleges, 42 theological seminaries, and 47 law schools, and we have not a single institution designed to furnish the agriculturist, the manufacturer, the mechanic, or the merchant, with the education that will prepare him for the profession to which his life is to be devoted."

Leaving these extracts, which our zeal for reform in popular education would gladly extend to the whole report, we close this part of our subject, with the observation, that the *peculiarities* in the course of instruction in Farmers' College is, that they do not require the study of the dead languages, or the pure mathematics, teaching both, however, to those who may choose, substituting therefor other branches having more direct relation to the practical duties of life, giving a diploma, or special certificate, of attainments, as the case may be, reducing the regular term from four to three years, and allowing a shorter or longer period as individuals may determine.

In answer to the inquiry, what are the wants of Farmers' College? it will be well briefly to sketch its past history and present state.

By the individual efforts of Freeman G. Cary, an academy was commenced at what is now called College Hill, six miles north of Cincinnati, in 1833, with eight pupils, which, in the course of that year, increased to twenty-four. The increase was gradual but constant. In 1838 it averaged over one hundred scholars, and continued increasing in numbers and the favor of the public. In 1846, Mr. Cary had invested upwards of $10,000 in grounds, buildings and apparatus, necessary for the well-being of his establishment, and "the cry was still they come," beyond his ability properly to teach. By this time about 700 persons had been more or less educated, and were applying their attainments successfully to the duties of life.

An appeal was then made to the public to increase the facilities for education at this point, by a subscription, in shares, of thirty dollars each, for the erection of a college edifice, to be held by an incorporation, which was obtained from the Legislature in the session of 1846–47, under the style of the "Farmers' College of Hamilton county."

The appeal was nobly responded to, funds were subscribed and paid so promptly, that in 1847–48, a beautiful and substantial building, 120 by 48 feet, three stories high, was erected on a pleasant and elevated site, containing about four acres of ground, the building in which we now are. Is it not evidence of a public appreciation of its objects? Over four hundred persons were contributors. A subscription was also made for a telescope, with which an excellent one, with an object glass of $6\frac{1}{4}$ inches in diameter, has been procured, and is in use.

Here was the incorporation, with its grounds, stone, brick, mortar, &c., faithfully, tastefully, and cheaply put together. There was Cary's Academy, "in the full tide of successful experiment," Mr. Cary a successful and popular teacher, a warm and ardent pioneer advocate for reform in the system of collegiate education indicated in this report, as his valedictory at taking leave of the college where he was educated, his writings, conversation, published and unpublished addresses during fourteen years, will abundantly demonstrate. The course of duty was too plain to be questioned, and after such legislation as was necessary and proper to make the institution subservient to the wished-for reform, to Mr. Cary was offered, and he accepted, the barren honor to carry out the plan. The trustees also regulated the payment of interest on the stock which was payable in tuition, so that there can be no accumulation of debt, considering the amount not applied in any year, a donation to the institution, which was confirmed at a subsequent meeting by the stockholders.

It has now been in operation nearly three years, the students numbering in 1848, 89 in the college proper, and 111 in the preparatory department; in 1849, 109 in the former, 113 in the latter: the faculty consisting of four professors, a teacher in ancient and modern languages, and principal of the preparatory school. The plan of instruction pursued is appreciated as being, on the score of general usefulness, in advance of other collegiate institutions, and a greater number have availed themselves of its advantages, than in any college in the west. To the casual observer, a high state of prosperity and increasing usefulness seems evident. And such undoubtedly would be the case, had not public munificence and private liberality so enriched and endowed other institutions, that education in all our colleges must be disposed of at far less than its cost.

In handing over the corporate property to Pres. Cary, as a corporation, we virtually said, take and use it as we have directed, pay insurance and the required interest on the stock, pay the salaries of professors, tutors and teachers such as we will approve, pay for apparatus, fuel, lights, and keep the property in thorough repair, receive the revenues for tuition and rent of dormitories,—what is left after paying for all these, is the salary you shall be entitled to. It is all we have. In President Cary's report to the Board of Trustees of the 27th March of the present year, he says:

"I think in the two and a half years already passed, a sufficiency of facts are furnished, greatly to aid in our future plans and efforts, perhaps such as may considerably modify our future action."

And what are the facts detailed in that report? After stating the injurious effects of the fear of cholera and small-pox, in 1849, which caused a short suspension of studies, he says:

"The attendance has been large the past winter, uniform health has prevailed, regularity and prosperity seem now to be completely restored, and we have numbered 160 the past term. Our professorships are all filled with men who I am hearty in saying are fully competent to the several stations, than with whom, I never labored with more satisfaction or surer confidence of success. There has been no revulsion, no withdrawal of confidence, no diminution of patronage. But the interests of the college have not been thus sustained, without great self-denial and personal sacrifice, more I am satisfied than this community will continue to require, more at least than they can for a long time reasonably expect."

Still farther, he says:

"You are ready to enquire, how has the college been kept up through these adverse circumstances, paid its professors, paid interest on the stock as demanded, insurance, fuel, lights, repairs, furniture, apparatus, &c., &c., and in these respects, kept them fully equal to other colleges, and at the same time not incurred a ruinous debt; this without endowment or any income, other than tuition fees, while all our colleges with endowments, tuition fees, and many perquisites, are in debt, some of them deeply. I answer, the college meets the exigencies of the times, is blessed with a numerous paying patronage, without which it could not exist a single day, for it depends on this entirely, and by the strict economy of all concerned. The professors live on small salaries, smaller than it is reasonable to ask men of such acknowledged abilities to live upon; $500 per year is now the highest given. They must pursue their avocations out of a love for science, or regard to those engaged in its prosecution,—perhaps for both of these united. As for myself, I may state that while I have $10,000 invested, say nothing of business tact, energy and reputation, which I value as worth something, I have been content with the pittance left, if any, and if none, by industry and strict economy, and the fruits of a few acres of ground, to eke out a bare support."

Mr. Cary makes no complaint, not expecting the attainment of so great an object without sacrifice, and says:

"Did I this day know that it would finally be successful, that a spirit would be awakened all over our land to put forth similar efforts, increasing the facilities and inspiring a desire for a more liberal mental training of the million, resulting in the proper modification of our colleges to suit the times, &c., &c., I would be willing not only that my money should be sacrificed, but my life's best energies spent, even to the close, in the accomplishment of such desirable results."

It will be seen that this institution as now conducted, is necessarily partly of a private character, liable to interruption whenever the former academy buildings, fixtures and apparatus, shall be withdrawn, which Mr. Cary has an undoubted right to do at any moment. It wants the means to purchase such of these as are necessary adjuncts to education at the college. It wants the means to place it upon a firm foundation as *a public institution*, beyond the fluctuations inseparable from mere individual enterprise.

It will also be seen that the revenues of the college are less than will sustain the requisite number of professors and teachers, who must be men of talent and ability, for the success of the institution depends upon it—that whatever is taught, be well taught—an increase of students will require more teachers, and not help the matter. As no reduction of expenses is possible, the plain obvious mode would seem to be to raise the price of tuition, which is now somewhat higher in ours than in colleges generally, which makes the matter a serious one. You ask, how is this? Which we answer by quoting from President Wayland's address before referred to.

"The demand for this kind of education, (preparation for the learned professions,) has decreased. It could not be disposed of for cost. The first effort made was to provide the means of furnishing it below cost. When it could not be sustained at this reduction, the next effort made was to furnish a large part of it gratuitously. Hence, if it be desired to render a college prosperous, we do not so much ask in what way we can afford the best education, or confer the greatest benefit on the community, but how can we raise funds, by which our tuition may be most effectually either reduced in price or given away altogether?"

"We have produced an article for which the demand is diminishing. We sell it at less than cost, and the deficiency is made up by charity. We give it away, and still the demand diminishes."

He illustrates the liberality with which education is supported, the cost to the public at which the present collegiate system is sustained, and the manner in which tuition fees are cheapened, by reference to the statistics of Harvard College for 1849.

"The amount of funds, according to the Report of the Treasurer of Harvard College, appropriated to the education of under-graduates, or the academic department, is $467,162.17. The interest of this sum, together with the fees for tuition, furnish the means of supporting the institution. This interest at six per cent. is $28,029.72; that is, the college pays out for education this amount more than it receives for tuition. If we divide the sum by the average number of graduates for ten years, (fifty-seven,) it will give $491.01, which is the portion received by every graduate. In other words, the public or private munificence of the friends of this noble institution, grant a bonus of $491 to every student who takes his regular degree.

"But this is only a portion of the amount invested in education. The lands, buildings, library, apparatus, museums, and other means of instruction for the benefit of the student, would probably amount to as large a sum as the fund above mentioned.

"If we add these together, we shall see that every graduate of this institution, in addition to all that he pays for his own education, costs the public nearly $1,000; and yet the Treasurer complains of the straightened condition of the University.

"Here then is a college situated in the centre of a most intelligent community, directed by gentlemen of public spirited benevolence, officered by scholars of the highest reputation, which, with such means at its command, finds it difficult to sustain itself. The fault is not in the community, nor in the instructors; it must be in the system, if there be a fault at all.

"By a similar comparison of the funds of the Law, Divinity and Medical Schools, with the present number of the senior class in each, it will appear that each law student receives from the fund, towards the payment of his education, $ 86; each medical student, $27; and each divinity student, $1680.

This last is larger for the present year, in consequence of the small number of the senior class. The cost of Theological education in our endowed seminaries, is probably about $1,000, besides whatever the student pays himself. This is the premium paid by the public on this branch of professional education."

Brown University, besides the buildings, library, and apparatus, has a fund of $34,300, the interest of which is applicable to repairs, and to lesson the cost of tuition in it. "The number of students, for several years, has not increased, but has diminished. Hence the condition of the institution has become embarrassed." No one would pretend there was any other cause for this, than the general apathy towards all the colleges.

So much for the *expense* to the community, at which the present system of collegiate education has been carried on. It is not of course to be presumed it is to the same extent in all our colleges: probably the average will be at some point between the two cases stated; none will be found without large endowments.

Miami University, at Oxford, in our own State, has the annual revenue of the interest on the sale of a township of land, (over 23,000 acres,) and that land exempted from taxation. Athens has even more land; both are in a state of exhaustion, and have instituted inquiries why they have so few students—why, when learning is considered more necessary than formerly, when the numbers who want, and the ability to obtain it, are so greatly increased—when learned and popular Presidents, Professors, and Instructors, have been appointed from any of the large sects, and from no particular sect—when they have diminished their expenses to the lowest possible amount, have exhausted their revenues, and contracted debts, to reduce the price of tuition, still hoping the tide would soon turn in their favor. An occasional wave may have brightened hope, but subsiding, it is found to ebb, ebb still. Some attribute this to political party bias, some to pro-slavery, others to abolition opinions, some to Calvinism, others to the want of it, some to too stringent, others to too lax government. After a few years it will probably be discovered that they are trying to sell what is not marketable,—not that it is useful *learning*, for that is in higher appreciation and demand than ever before,—but the by-gone, stale, dead languages, worth something truly as an ornament, but not necessary, or even highly useful, in the bustling, busy, and exciting battle of life.

We have but to refer the public to the catalogue and course of study of the Farmers' College, to show the important and radical difference between this and all other institutions of learning. A minimum course of study is prescribed, and this course, or its *equivalent*, must be thoroughly mastered before a pupil can receive the Diploma of the College. But by the introduction of equivalents, it will be observed, that a young man, otherwise promising, may secure the honors of the institution with a less amount of attainment in any given department, provided that, in another department, he has progressed beyond the prescribed limit.

A course of education, liberal and thorough, suited to the genius of our government, our people, and our age; an education which embodies in it the very elements of the growth and stability of our institutions, and based upon the principle that the masses are to rule, is the education which we propose to furnish..

An institution like ours can be more nearly supported by tuition fees, because there will be no lack of pupils, and the tuition may be somewhat higher—not enough higher, however, under present circumstances, to make it pay its own way. Collegiate instruction has been so long sold for less than cost, that the people expect it at the quotations.

As it may not be obvious to all, why the matter of education may not be safely left to individual enterprise, we would observe, that the duties of life are so various, as to require for proper instruction in them a division of labor among professors and teachers, requisite for high attainments, and for facility in imparting it, so that the services of many persons, with a large outlay of capital in grounds, buildings, chemical, philosophical, astronomical, and other apparatus, library, and other appendages, are required; the collection, combination, and application of which, are entirely beyond the scope of individual enterprise. Even were individuals competent to it, the institution would want that permanency which is attained by an incorporation, or legal person, having perpetual succession. Hence the absolute necessity, in all civilized countries, of permanent institutions of learning.

It will now be plain what is wanted, and the reason why it is wanted. We want the means to purchase such of the contiguous grounds, academy buildings, fixtures, and apparatus, as may be necessary, and also, an endowment, the interest or income of which, shall be appropriated to the several professorships, granting to each a certain stipend, not to make a sinecure, but to insure a possibility to live. The balance of the salaries to depend, after the payment of all other necessary expenses, by some just and equitable rule, which the Trustees might establish, upon the income for tuition. The corporation have no other means to appropriate to these objects, and should not under any circumstances incur a debt. This, it is believed, would attract the best class of professors and teachers. They would be brought directly into salutary contact with the public, and the extent of their remuneration depend upon industry and skill in their profession.

To attain these objects, we cannot suppose a less sum than forty to fifty thousand dolllars would well answer.

More than this could be used to advantage, in extending the library and apparatus of the institution.

We are well satisfied that there is abundant means, and willing hearts, to contribute to this fund, and that the country will be enriched and otherwise blessed by the benefaction. Should there be a partiality for particular professorships, or a desire that particular branches be taught, such preference might be indicated with the donation, which the trustees would be bound to respect. In this way a foundation might be laid for new studies, and for increased usefulness.

Consider an institution of learning, the directory elected triennially, by a thousand or more contributors to its funds, stimulated by a desire for the application of its benefits and advantages to their own sons, or to the general diffusion of knowledge; having the fundamental or iniatory professorships endowed, so far as to attract those best qualified to teach, and to give permanence and stability to their action; with a provision for the foundation of particular professorships, such as present wants and future discoveries, in the spiritual, mental, and physical worlds, may require, none of which to be captiously objected to, where public or private liberality manifests their importance, by placing them above a necessary participation in the common fund; founded with a desire of beneficence, by free-will offerings, their use measured and sustained by freedom in receiving or rejecting their instructions, *a University in harmony with our other institutions.* Bigotry and party might combine to establish what could do no harm, while the Christian, the patriot, the utilitarian, and the friend of progress, to perform what would result in incalculable good. How many persons, living and dying, who yearn with the desire to spread knowledge among men, by the legacy of means insufficient of themselves to perpetuate their objects, might here appropriate their bounty to the general, or particular object of their choice.

This brings us to the final inquiry, what are the claims of Farmers' College? It is rather in sorrow than exultation, that we are obliged to plead the excusiveness of its claims upon public beneficence and liberality. We should rejoice to see many like competitors for public favor. It is the foundation or nucleus of a most noble institution, at exactly the time and place for an enlarged sphere of usefulness, in which more than four hundred fathers have evinced an interest by their subscription to make it what it is. It is situated in a most healthful, picturesque and pleasant locality, airy and unconfined, with room for any desirable increase; in a well settled, intelligent, and fast increasing neighborhood, easy of access from all points, and as near the most populous city of the West, as will comport with a due regard to health and morals—and pledged, as its name implies, to provide instruction to the largest class of producers, but limited in providing it to none. By its charter, the contributors to its funds choose tri-annually from their number fifteen trustees or directors, who control and direct the application of its funds. So far, they have been selected of all parties and shades of opinion, and may continue to be, so as to secure the institution against undue sectarian or party bias. It stands forth the first public embodiment of a reform in collegiate education, required by us as Christians, as friends of progress, and the social elevation of all ranks and pursuits. It is an institution eminently calculated to dignify and exalt labor,—where any class of producers, the votaries of any science, the friends of the arts, the advocates of ancient or modern literature,—any and all classes and pursuits, may endow professorships, and have teachers, to impart instruction to those disposed and willing to receive it. It is an institution where we may send our sons to learn, under necessary qualifications, *what we choose, all that we choose*, and *nothing but what we choose.* Nearly a thousand young men already rejoice in the advantages

4

they have received from it, including the incipient stages of its progress.

The good it may be made the means of accomplishing, can only be measured by the possible elevation of literature, capacity for instruction, the requirements of science, and the blessings of religion.

So far as relates to a reformation in the course of instruction in our time-honored institutions of learning, it may seem presumption in us to speak as we have. But it is in the order of things, that when the venerable and wide-spreading king of the forest has out-lived its usefulness, the *worm* attacks and carries to its vitals the agents of decomposition, causing slow but sure decay—and it must give place to a growth more vigorous, and of greater present and future usefulness.

Respectfully submitted, in behalf of the Commitee.

G. RICHARDS.

ELLAND, Butler Co. O., June 12, 1850.

www.ingramcontent.com/pod-product-compliance
Lightning Source LLC
LaVergne TN
LVHW011140110826
845150LV00008B/2427

* 9 7 8 1 4 1 8 1 9 2 8 7 7 *